TO$$ IT UP Production'$

CAN YOU RELATE?

Written By: FREAKY DEE

Copyright 2025 DarrinDLacyJunior
All Rights Reserved

The Urban Story: My Dreams Are Free, But The Hustle Is Sold Separately: Ya Dig!

I'd like to honestly Thank God personally for my praying Granny Jo, Paw-Paw Herb T. & Granny B. C., there's no relation too powder, I thought I should mention that myself.); I'd honestly like to inform y'all by apologizing towards my God, because even I know God isn't through with me just yet: Ya Dig!

Warning: I pray that all of my readers, hearers, and doers, you know those of you who have a great fantasy/imagination and understanding as well, I just Pray that y' all have a great read; Ya Dig!

Now I would like to give a very special Thank You too Shameka Jones, Marinette Beal, Rick Chettman & Native Book Publishing; Ya Dig!

Genre: Erotica Fiction Romance Novel

All of the names, characters, and incidents depicted in this novel are products of the author's imagination or are used factiously.

Any resemblance to actual events, locales, organizations, or persons, living or deceased, is entirely coincidental, and beyond the intent, of the author and publisher.

Acknowledgments

To Momma T. Y. B, Pop's Los, Siblings: Jick, Rea-Rea, Neek, Na-Na, Sakey & Freddy; listen: Big Bro ain't got nothing but Love for each of Y' all BAD A$$E$, Uncle Greg, Joc & Murda, look stop fighting just for my attention, now I Love each of my in-laws also: Ya Dig!

Now my work has probably taken, as long as it's taken, only because I probably edit my manuscript a million times if not more; but God I am so sorry, because I'm not here to please anyone else except for you, Lord Jesus, now I do understand you're most definitely pleased with all of my services; Ya Dig!

Full Series/Book One

Dedication

Anesha Green, Eddie Paul Dowdy, Josie Biggurs, Arthur & Audrey Phillips, Rev. LD & Thelma Thomas, Carlton Scoot, Joyce Ann Brown, Joyce Burks, Jeremey West, Myrtis Boyd, Joseph Ingram, Brandi Hall, Eric King, Karla Thomas, Calvin Robison, Katoya Shelby.

Synopsis

Kyle Dixon 29, who often go by his street recognition which is KD, or then again, known by majority of the ladies by his stage name: "Freaky Dee": I mean I don't know exactly how you may take of him, but I advise y' all to do as the Bible say, which is literally: Judge Not That Ye Be Not Judged!

Contents

Chapter One: Pussy Whipped!.. 1

Chapter Two: Man In Me! 5

Chapter Three: You Don't Say! 8

Chapter Four: It's Better Too Be Seen /Than To Be Viewed!11

Chapter Five: My Inner Thought's! 14

Chapter Six: Damn-Damn-Damn!...17

Chapter Seven: Reminiscing! 20

Chapter Eight: Clean Up Woman! 23

Chapter Nine: If Only You Knew? 27

Chapter Ten: Woosah! 30

Chapter Eleven: It'll All Come Out In The Wash! 33

Chapter Twelve: Good Morning Wood! 37

Chapter Thirteen: These Mannish Thought's! 40

Chapter Fourteen: A Virtuous Woman! 43

Chapter Fifteen: Ashes Too Ashes 47

Chapter Sixteen: Corporation!...50

Chapter Seventeen: Choose, Lose or be Confused! 53

Chapter Eighteen: Jezebel Spirit! 56

Chapter Nineteen: Hay Is For Horses! 59

Chapter Twenty: Leave Me Be! 62

Chapter Twenty-One: Back To Normalcy! 65

Chapter Twenty-Two: Welfare Check! 68

Chapter Twenty-Three: I Am Not Ashamed! 71

About the Author 75

Chapter One: Pussy Whipped!

I literally couldn't deny myself of being, Wifey Anesha couldn't deny herself of being dickmatized, look whatsoever it was, we're literally hooked on each other's Love; that's my story and I'm sticking to it, Ya Dig, I barely understood what could've transpired, when we're still considered as newlyweds.

Now I don't wanna blame it all on myself or anything, I informed her I wasn't the exact same little boy, as I use to be; I mean it isn't as if she's never been my clientele, I mean she knew I came from an entire family with Big Dick Energy, and we aren't all necessarily from the Harry Hines Blvd: Ya Dig.

With me already being a Head Pastor in charge, as well still a entrepreneur, and her being one of Dallas's finest beauticians/locticians, she didn't want another Woman in my head doing my dreads; if I'm not mistaken, she side-eyed me, when she first learned it's my Sister, who introduce me to dreads.

You see my Sister own's her very own Beauty Salon, it wasn't as if I was just sitting between a random female gapped open legs or something, I mean she has her cosmetology license; I guess she felt more comfortable with her own Sister in Love, becoming her very own personal beautician/makeup artist.

As I'm sure, y' all probably already know how most siblings are well known for keeping secrets from each other, so I know we're not alone; I wouldn't get myself upset, by running my blood pressure up, if I discovered Monte' still been deep sea diving with Anesha, nawl then again, I just hope I wouldn't.

If the Lord see fit to break up this happy home, I'm sure he wouldn't allow no kind's of foolishness or jealousy divide our Brotherly Bond; I seriously Love me some Anesha, and well I'm pretty sure she Love her some Kyle, see on Valentines day we did vow to Love each other, until death do us apart.

Now we're always cuddled up, I don't see why we won't finally downsize, because all it looks like is I pay an extremely high ass mortgage for only 3 people; what's so crazy is she won't even give me a baby, well not like I want, that was our agreement we agreed upon, before exchanging wedding vows.

I normally don't make a big fuss when I hear her and her so-call bestie, lounging around arguing, cussing and fussing up a storm, oh did I mention; I sit in my home office, and study the word of God, because it isn't as if I don't know my Bible inside out, I get a new translation every time I reread it.

Who am I kidding, I mean I know her so-call bestie Aquakneesha, probably had the hugest crush on me, and well that's hand's down; no offense or anything, but isn't that usually how all Women are, especially whenever it come's down too a Pastor, I don't mean to necessarily look or sound conceited.

I just so happen to have my own insecurities or whatnot, Wifey seem to be the only person I know of, well other than myself having a problem with my own bare feet; I mean I always kiss, lick and suck her feet or toes, but whenever time comes for her to return the favor, she always find some kind of excuse.

But I take it she doesn't want to insult my bare feet, I mean I clearly understand I'm a Man and all, then again, I use to pay for her feet; shouldn't she owe my feet some kind of affection, no offense but I know she doesn't want me glancing at another Woman for the exact same affection, I seek from her.

Lord, I see why it be so much animosity after Church, specially on Sunday evenings, a Man of God can't even get a full-course Dinner, well not less I pay for it myself; I do obviously try best not to curse so much nowadays, but if I don't entertain the devil, then she'd never leave me be, or then even flee.

Honestly I can't blame anyone except for myself, well then again, God created me in his image, so I understand why I'm attractive towards the opposite sex; I tell you now Jimmy Choo, isn't my only reason, I'm not as materialistic, well not as some people tend to call me, right to my own face, I'm not.

I'm just glad they always catch me at the right place, only because my armor-bearer's won't allow me to get out of character while at "The Sanctuary Missionary Baptist Church"; those are like my Brother's From Another Mother, see God placed it upon my heart, to even trust all of them equally.

So we're close as in Bro's, I mean they'd do for me, as I'd do for them, I suppose you can automatically call each of them my support system; then again, we do try our very best, not to date each other women on purpose, it isn't like we run trains like we use to, when we were young bucks coming up!

Chapter Two: Man In Me!

By me being considered a Grown Man, my hygiene must be on point, I mean I don't expect a Woman to automatically show pity for me, because I wouldn't be able to show pity if it was vice versa; I'd Love for my Wifey to be on point, I mean that's my reason for even marrying The One God Chose For Me.

I mean, I was already exhausted, and I wondered exactly what I could do, instead of just tapping out suddenly, which only put me in mind of Mark Nelson's song "15 Minutes; I doubted it wouldn't be my fault, my problem or even my situation I'd ever have to experience, but then again, to each is his own.

From Anesha point view, I'm not perfect, but then again, my heart is pure, ladies don't call me "Freaky Dee" for nothing, hopefully, Wifey doesn't spill any tea about these unexpected quickies; especially to her ol gossiping/messy ass clientele, that normally be at her Beauty Salon, early in the a-m.

Anesha, know's I suffer from a-d-h-d, marijuana calm my nerve, I mean there's no shame in my game, not when I'm doing my thang; it wasn't storming, but I couldn't help overhearing a siren, from my tongue, wiggling deep in her pussy, I try keeping her from climbing the walls, but I wasn't too assured.

I knew positively, Wifey couldn't be considered a lesbian, which I heard off up in these streets, because I knew their wasn't a strap better or bigger, what am I saying, guess I am conceited; she admire my hoochie daddy shorts that I rock, couldn't help noticing my dick, so her pussy, couldn't be tamed.

You could automatically notice by the piercing stare in her eyes, she probably had a mouth full to say, she just didn't know exactly how to comprehend; I was already thinking and waiting for her dry-ass arguments to begin, she wanted me to Door dash, Uber Eats or Zelle a restaurant call: "Nana B's".

With me reminiscing about her legs being gapped apart, I don't know how I managed to forget about it, but I should've reminisced how she look when she about to squirt; because it shot me all in my face, and if I couldn't swim, then I most definitely shouldn't have tried impersonating, no damn Trey Songz.

While she's waiting on supposedly an important phone call from her so-call gynecologist, I tried my best keeping her spirits lifted; I guess she tried exposing herself to me before I found out anything, and you know how these random streets are, they're gossipers, which involves he messy ass clientele.

Look, I'm just not that gullible, not enough to believe everything I hear, I'm not, because these random streets don't know half the bs they're gossiping about, y'all know I'm not lying; rather it's said in random barber shops, beauty salons, ratchet ass car washes, or even different Church parking lots.

When she got the call, she'd been waiting on, first they congratulated her, her results were positive, she just needed to reschedule, she didn't understand why she'd been feeling discombobulated lately, but she just knew, it'd be good news from here on out, not only was she anxious, but also impatient.

I knew better, so I did better. Wifey try rushing out. I knew she wanted to stop by her gynecologist herself. I made her some homemade waffles, she rushed out; lucky me, I knew how to take a quick hoe bath. I haven't done it since I was the main attraction. I know I'm not the only Man done it before.

Ever since the nurse informed her, her results were indeed positive, she just knew she'd soon be experiencing morning sickness; what she didn't know or even recognize, was that wasn't all she'd be experiencing, she began losing patches of hair, if she wasn't a beautician, she'd literally be fucked.

Something told me, Wifey gone trip about my ringtone, Bro hasn't called or page me yet, I don't need him calling giving Wifey assumptions I'm cheating; because nine times out of ten, that's exactly where her mind is anyways, I wouldn't dare get myself caught up like I'm still young, dumb and full of cum.

I tried calling Bro to find out his eta, he was bumping Trapboy Freddy: "Lil Quita" in the background; I asked where he was, he inform me, that he was in route to come to scoop me up, I ask why hadn't he paged me just yet, he couldn't even explain, but I don't know why he say he felt like a squatter.

Usually, I return his page, I didn't need him calling my phone, because 112 Player instantly plays whenever I receive a incoming call, knowing it's a RED FLAG; I tried explaining it was my jam, shi-i-it Wifey wasn't trying to hear it, I did the best thing possible, she heard my feet screech in of our foyer!

Chapter Three: You Don't Say!

See, I didn't know it was quite possible anybody could cause me to react like she does, so I quickly blamed it on my inner feelings, well I think I do anyway; I guess she figure, I had a change of clothes at work, she sent me out in my hoochie daddy shorts, isn't she like exposing my goods to the world.

Now I had the slightest idea, who's bikini I'd been stretching, knowing damn well I can't fit any larges, I mean, I wouldn't be leaving skid marks in my bikini anyway; she says all I seem to do is overthink myself, I only sense a stranger been in my house, I ain't been buying no damn bikini's lately anyway.

My conscience couldn't help but overhear the speaker blast: Shirley Murdock: "As We Lay", I mean I couldn't help but visualize; I know I shouldn't play evil for evil but wait until one of her clientele call to schedule an appointment, they'll have to be properly reintroduced to who, yours truly: "Freaky Dee".

Now I clearly understand, I'm exactly what they may call an uncut Brotha after all, I try my damndest to keep my hygiene on point, and acceptable towards all Females, including The One God Chose For Me; I don't know what she'd do to me, if I came home with a dirty or even stinky dick for example.

Anesha's known for keeping my turtleneck squeaky clean, I believe she was a cat in another life, that or her nickname once was Jawbone; I can't hate her fetishes, I pray she wasn't Lorena Bobbitt, see all I do is offer myself to her through sickness, and health from this day forward, until death do us apart.

I'm not the only Mandingo embarrassed of having to sprint, no jot to the bathroom, because those farts I been secretly letting go of, turns out to be diarrhea after all; I just pray I make a safe landing, this the main reason I took hoe baths, back in the day, I was like MC Hammer, "2 Legit 2 Quit".

I already don't like exposing too much toe cleavage, or even my long ass toes perse', I had gout as a teen, but as I find myself being head of my household, I don't mind walking around barefooted; it's pathetic when your toes and toenails blend in with your wood-stain floor, and hopefully I'm not alone.

Thanks to Gramps, he's the late-Rev. I always wanted to be like when I was a young Buck coming up, I don't know how, but that's where my bowleggedness came from; God, please forgive me for speaking out of turn, but ladies in his congregation, really didn't receive the Holy Ghost, they we're just luring.

Wifey already has these wig heads surrounding our house, I know Anesha probably trying to set me up for failure, but that's where my multitasking skill come in; I play it off as I sashay around my crib, I mean she never say a mumbling word, so I don't mind exposing my feet when we're home alone.

I mean, it was like Wifey saw a complete ghost or something, I didn't want to start any commotion with her, I let her know I took out the garbage; I informed her I told Bro, he could swing by and scoop me up, I knew he needed a designated driver, she already know I'm like my Bro's one and only keeper.

For some awkward reason or whatnot, she wasn't trying to go to her gynecologist after all, she assume she knew exactly what they're gone tell her, you see that didn't sit quite right with me, she said it's her hemorrhoids as usual, and that I was a Man, so therefore, I shouldn't be knowing a female's anatomy.

I don't know if she trying to pull the wool over my eyes, by sneaking a unknown caller in my crib, but I'm getting to the bottom of this bs, wait till my Bro get's here; I don't know what it is, Wifey trying her damnedest to belittle me or something, I ain't ever been in trouble with the law, I been GANG-GANG.

Wifey, trying her damnedest to belittle me or something, or raise Ike, if not Mister characters if not Lazarus from a shallow grave; I don't necessarily mean to jeopardize the alphabetical order community, but what the Lord has for me is for me, that's my story and well I'm sticking to it, Ya Dig.

We been going on and on, about these yeast infection bikinis, she wants to bring her Bro who's been incarcerated since I don't know when; I mean she prepared me a stiff drank, I ain't gone waste good liquor like that, I know she want me to forget about it, but I'm not even that gullible or tipsy just yet.

I thought I just heard 3 knocks at the front door, Aquakneesha who's supposedly on her way to get a phonytail, instead of her usual lace front; you'd swear she: Willona, from Good Times, that or the infamous Gossip To Go With Flo from K104, they gossip the same, with her scandalous messy ass!

Chapter Four: It's Better Too Be Seen /Than To Be Viewed!

Time I reach the front door, that drank I'd been chugging, snuck upon me, had my head spinning in different directions, sure y'all know, I expose my Voice to Barry White; I know she heard the slur in my: Who It Be? That's when she start hyperventilating, now what stripper y'all know, has that effect?

I noticed Bro tried his best to ease in behind her, Aquakneesha was already starstruck while coming to herself humming "Fantasia: Free Yourself", wearing tightly fitted knickerbockers, matching halter top, sockless & white K-Swiss; she's watched Clueless one too many times, she had, Dionne down to a T.

Honestly, God has Blessed us with all our senses, I mean I literally couldn't help but recognize her camel toe puckering up; I mean don't you just hate it when you automatically start repenting before committing whatsoever sin, you know you're about to commit, just because you feel it coming alone.

I notice that drank I been chugging, had me feeling sluggish, you know ready to lay it on down, but my dick was finally saluting; Aquakneesha and I shared a warm embrace, something didn't sit right with me though, it felt as if I was bear hugging my own lil Bro, because I notice her dick saluting also.

Now is she a true BBW, or was she just trying her best to manipulate me, Wifey better hurry up and get home, before Uncle Luke escapes Freaky Dee's mind; all I need is one more strong-ass drank, and normally lil Bro drives me, or better yet lures me to dranking, that's just why I Gotta Be More Careful.

I glance around, to see if I had an audience, I said "Oh, so you one of those, she already wore Rainbow contacts; she blushed, cut her eyes at me, I don't know what I did to turn it on, but I didn't wanna leave Bro out, so we all hug, I was trying my best to reminisce of what Wifey mentioned before leaving.

I know she said: It's nice to be important/but also important to be nice, I know It's Better To Be Seen/Than To Be Viewed, but why do I hear sirens; why are helicopters flying above my head as if I'm gone run, I must be hallucinating if not high, that's my conscience I hear, it ain't like we've negotiated.

Some people find it bizarre, I no longer have a Man cave anymore, my knucklehead Bro is always showing up drunk as a skunk, so it's his sober-up corner for now; I don't wanna go off on him, he's one of those suicidal mofo's, but if only he kills himself again, it ain't gone be no more resuscitating.

Before I could warn him, he whipped out his Splackavellie approach on Cousin It, I know I was in the wrong, I should've warned him to check her throat, that drank snuck up on me, we couldn't help noticing her camel toe, not 3rd leg winking, I'm looking to have a good time, I'll just tell him in the a.m.

Then again, I'm sure he's probably run into more than a couple TS's being employee of the month at "Dicks Sporting Goods; now everybody happen to Love my new house aroma, only because I bought an Instant Fountain off TV late one night, it's been my lifesaver ever since, it first arrived in the mail.

I couldn't control being antisocial. Monte ask if it's any more Kool-Cups. I laugh it off and told him this wasn't a Kool-Cup; this a Grown Man drank. He ask if it's anymore. I glance at Aquakneesha. She said, "That's a Vegas Bomb or a frozen Hurricane". Those drank's known for catching me off guard.

Suddenly, Bro got real bubbly eyed, before grinning and nodding his head at me, with this gigantic fake ass smirk plastered on his face, he ask me if I knew exactly what he was thinking; now we came from the exact same Pussy, as well as the same Nut Sac, but I don't know why I was fidgeting so.

Instead of Bro using new lines, he was more interested in picking up some type of birth control, Brand Name and most defiantly not generic; but Bro just may be mentally challenged, but the one thing he isn't has to be foolish, he most definitely don't look like what he's been through, I can vouch for that.

We invited Aquakneesha on the patio, but I ain't too proud to beg, I know Wifey has these hidden cameras installed, well that's one of the particular destinations they're installed; ooh shit, I won't look directly into the camera, fool me once, shame on you, fool me twice, shame on me, I just need a nut.

Honestly, at times I can't stand it, I be so fucking horny nowadays, that's what I shouldn't have to be, not if I have a devoted Wifey-RIGHT; I mean I do hear those naysayers about my marriage, I can hear them now: "Run Forrest, Run", but I'm not leaving my Wifey, there just has to be something wrong!

Chapter Five: My Inner Thought's!

See I Love Wifey with all my heart, and I believe, she Loves me the same, I can't stand being a nympho, I wish I could have sex just as much as I breathe; I know I must get tired at some point; I'm trying best to remember when she fucked up in the past, I need a pass, this might be that pass I need.

Some people assume us Husbands, don't worry about our Wife throughout our days, but if we're too busy making payments on mortgages; no, I don't have jealous bones in my body, but with her being so fucking suspicious about me, she got cheating, rattling & scandalous bones all throughout her body.

Now I don't have time for scouting out her Beauty Salon, only because not only do that give out stalker vibes, but I'm not that crazy, well then again, I'm Crazy In Love with my Queen of course; but I need to make some coffee, on my KEURIG, so I can calm down, maybe I can go and shoot pool with my Bro.

"Holdup," where Bro ease off too, where the Hell Aquakneesha, I went to what suppose to be my Bro's sober-up corner, I didn't expect to find what I found out, but my Bro turns out to be fluid after all; well, I didn't think he'd be okay with running a train on a trainee, I guess we all got secrets then, huh?

Bro was holding his ankles, allowing Aquakneesha analogize him, I knew it look sort of gayish, Hell, sorry to inform y' all, but I was up next; I mean I know I've been secretly farting up a storm, but when she got ready to insert her tongue in my rectum, who would've known the bubble guts, were up next.

Although it was quite embarrassing, I kept it 100% Playa, I mean I couldn't burst out laughing for instance, that's a hard pill for me to swallow, I'm sure I'm not alone; shi-i-it I ain't gotta lie, that fart was so dangerous it damn near smeared her mascara, obviously bozo, the clown look better than her.

She's considered a butter face, because everything look's good but her face, I mean I can hear my conscience trying to gossip about her camel toe as of now; she already know damn well, what she's doing to me, now Monte' is our parent's only weak link child, and what the Hell, she's got him sprung.

It don't feel right, holding secrets from Wifey, not that I know her best friend Aquakneesha is so much better at fellatio than she is; I mean I could tell Aquakneesha where she got that no gagging reflex from, one thing for sure, I wouldn't ever want to distract a person while they're doing such a great job.

Now I have the slightest idea, why she chose Bro over me, maybe because I'm still uncircumcised, and he's circumcised, what y'all thank; perhaps she & Wifey we're closer friends than I thought they were, she didn't want to overstep her boundary, now if Women can do it, then why can't us Men even try.

You could tell, I was doing something wrong, I mean I was so fucking paranoid, I mean I couldn't even hold up my own iPhone long enough to snap a quick picture, or even a snippet; I guess I got myself a quick view for my eyes only, I can't argue with myself about what I happened to see with my own eyes.

They moved Wifey's Peloton bike to the side, I wish they would've been courteous enough to move my pool table over, the exact same way, so I wouldn't have to clarify anything with anybody; Aquakneesha offered me fellatio, but I just need to know of any Man willing to pass up the opportunity of fellatio.

That alone, let's me know ahead of time, she wasn't concerned, or upset about my farting incidents, from her point of view, I'm a human being, I shouldn't be so shy; now obviously, I can be myself, and as of a matter fact, it's like she's one of the Homies, Hell, so don't come for us, if we don't send for ya.

Though she hadn't confessed with her mouth, she's a hermaphrodite, meaning she use to be a Man, I can't help but roeminisce what I mistakenly saw earlier; I'm not arrogant enough to know who's the Biggest, Fattest or Longest, Wifey and I aren't judgmental, I couldn't help peeking for my own ego.

Seriously, I hate to be the barrier of bad news, Aquakneesha don't have anything on me, I didn't think she did anyways, but why do she have me wondering like this; I know I'm not gay, why am I so infatuated: am I trying to creep on the low, I know it's considered infidelity, but why am I feening?

It isn't as if I didn't already know: A double-minded Man is unstable in all of his ways, therefore, I know Accept What God allows; and if I do just so happen to cheat on my Wifey, that would obviously mean I'm being too greedy for my very own goods, and that's also known as being very stingy too!

Chapter Six: Damn-Damn-Damn!

Maybe, if I spark a blunt while in the house, then on second thought, Wifey know I entertain guests on the patio, I wouldn't dare try jeopardizing Wifey asthma-like that; I know how she feels about smoke being in our house, and my back is too bad, to be slumbering on a couch for a night, if not several.

I know I'm not claustrophobic, but I try best to clean up everything before Wifey discovers anything, well anything out the ordinary; she swear up and down her time finally permitted her to speak, she know sex isn't the only thing on my mind, I was born and raised in the gutter, oops I meant the ghetto.

Damn-Damn-Damn, now here I am wondering how to disable these cameras, on second thought, knowing me I'd be done forgotten how to enable them again; isn't this the exact suspicious foolery I'm upset with Wifey about now, see I've got Playa all in my genes, I just know Daddy was a rolling Stone.

Man, I got too many aliases, oops, here I am snitching on myself, you know they say the Darker the berry, sweeter the juice, bet that's why I'm so fucking allergic now; I mean I can eat pussy daily, but I can't eat a pussy with a dick attached, if that's fluid, then I'm sorry, but I can't see myself being fluid.

I don't mean to let Bro down necessarily, he cool with whatsoever floats his boat, if Wifey don't want to break me off with something proper; then I got all rights to go wherever I'm needed or better yet wanted, I mean I can't help it Aquakneesha is where I'm needed and wanted, I'm not homophobic.

After pressing my key fob, and jumping into my BMW, I knew for a fact Aquakneesha would at least want to get in on the passenger side, but she chose to get chauffeured by her knights in shining armor; I don't even know when Bro and I filled out these applications, for these specific positions anyway.

So here we are pulling up to Williams, my idea was to get myself a 3-piece dark all legs, fries, strawberry soda, and poppers; June bug loaded up on Magnum's, our client was interested in Frooties, I had the slightest idea what she trying to expose, but we both got something she can suck on.

It was by what she did to enlighten us both, she all about that head game, now we're too damn grown to still be playing with a damn joystick; back when we were young bucks coming up, I was the smart ass, I was the bowlegged scammer, I always had to be stacking paper, however, or whenever I could.

Although we around the corner from the house, I couldn't help myself but hear a loud sound of an ambulance siren headed in our direction; my body tensed up and got numb, for some reason, but I couldn't stop having these anxiety attacks, and flashbacks of Nesha, but I'm sure that's not for her.

I'm glad I can reminisce, Nesha gone to her gynecologist, I know when she get home, she'll be exhausted, we can catch up on Netflix and chill; but I don't understand why I have a guilty conscience, I mean I already told y'all I'm a Nympho already, I can't help sex is what's constantly on my mind.

It's my senses that keeps both me and my dick in the world of trouble, I mean he's the one who give Ladies weird thoughts, well about me I mean him anyway; now I don't mean to necessarily say I'm nobodies Casanova, but I'm nobodies sugar Daddy, well my Wifey's, so please just ignore the ringtone.

My conscience make me feel guilty as sin, I mean I understand my flesh wants to commit adultery, but I haven't stepped outside my boundary; this ring on my ring finger only reminds me of what I already have, Lord, you Blessed us beyond our faults, I spoke it to the atmosphere, so have your way, O God.

That's when I got a notification from Methodist, letting me know my Wife flatlined twice, should they just continue resuscitating her? I guess she placed me on her emergency contact list, it's either that, or she has her husband listed, but I know how misery only loves company, so I wouldn't be surprised.

Aquakneesha, cause me to feel more and more like a hoe everyday, by dropping $50 here and there, like nuggets, on the edge of my dresser, everybody know how hoes get paid; I mean I don't want to fuck, it try it's best to seduce me with money, and everybody know: money is the root of all evil.

It isn't as if I don't remember Daddy teaching us as young bucks coming up, "Pimping Ain't Easy" sons, so as a Male Specimen; I had to go ahead pop my collar, which as Daddy would have normally done, right about now anyhow, I just swallowed my pride. And it said: Daddy, I just Love your energy!

Chapter Seven: Reminiscing!

Hypothetically, it cause me to get curious myself, I mean I couldn't help but fantasize about Wifey being knocked up by a hard knock-ass thug; so here I go wondering if he satisfied her better than me, he or she could obviously be the cause of her untiming illness, hopefully, it didn't affect me though.

I can't help being vulnerable at this point, I mean in one ear, I hear the Lord & I have a full-fledged conversation, God ask: Who shall I send? And who will go for us? I said here I am, send me, Satan knows, I'm vulnerable at this point, guess Satan felt okay with me being seduced by Aquakneesha.

By it kissing my earlobe, as well as down my neck, I couldn't pretend as if it didn't remind me of Wifey, I wonder how did it discover exactly where my hot spots were, oh yeah, I damn near forgot, it's Nesha gossiping ass clientele, because I knew exactly what I knew, I mean I can't call it a he or a she.

It allowed us both to know, normally it's considered a nudist, but what shall it profit a man if he gain the world and loses his soul, we already come from a functional but dysfunctional family as is; and eating ain't cheating, as well as sucking ain't fucking, so we ain't doing nothing, I don't need all of that.

Why don't y'all ride to Methodist with me, I mean you got people dying, that ain't ever died before, I don't know if it's my slightly bowlegged legs; my 32 pearly whites, my full chocolate lips, I think I'm having a panic attack, I hear it say "Take Your Time Young Man", so I can't be sexually frustrated.

Wifey always said: You know we're living on borrowed time, I never understood where she was headed, I don't need her 1-million-dollar insurance policy; I just want my Wifey back, Aquakneesha let me know she's here for me, I forgot she wasn't even what God created her to be, so I was just grieving.

Come hell or high water, I Love Women with my whole heart, this Broad blurts out and inform me: what am I gone do for Don's family, who often ran errands for your Wife?" see I never been so gullible before. Now, I will do just that if it wants to be addressed as a Woman. She has my utmost respect.

She noticed I been grieving. And she knew I probably wasn't feeling her quite like she wanted me to, but she started rubbing and squeezing my pecs and nipples. Then, moans out: Odysseus, that's all I've ever needed in my life, but instead, he wanted your girl Nesha—oops, I meant your common-law Wife.

I spoke out: I'm just glad I got my gun license, Aquakneesha side-eyed me saying for what: everybody already know, you all bark and no bite, I thought about it, she may be telling the truth; these compliments, I been receiving from her, I know I couldn't wait to become a widower for some reason.

The only reason, I even have mirrors mounted on my bedroom ceiling, is so I'd be able to wink at myself, whenever I'm dickmatizing my clientele or giving them the business, Ya Dig; I appreciate Wifey for checking out at her appointed timing, I guess this'll be Bro and I penthouse.

Now I know we should've been on at least an episode of "First 48, but Daddy said: son's "Pimping Ain't Easy", and Birds of a Feather Flock together, I'd never turn my back on

Bro; even though he paid close attention, so I can't do anything but fall in line, maybe he can help me find an acceptable Wife.

Then again: I saw what floats his boat, I guess I need to be more and more like him each and every day, hell nawl, I'm not a pathological liar: I'm gone be needing me a life alert button, putting up with the shenanigans he got, I guess I'm in a peculiar situation, truth be told, I Love myself more than that.

With me noticing, that was a Female's Urination Device not an actual dick, I'm just telling y'all now my dick has been confused ever since; However, I'd like to cater and cook for this chick, suddenly anyway, it's no wonder why she addicted to my type of boneless chicken & Hurricanes.

Aquakneesha explained she been borderline tomboyish all her life, she wanted everything Anesha had, which also included me once upon a time; I mean I tried my best to be a perfect gentleman, by looking and sounding as if I was surprised, it worked itself out in the end, because she met lil Bro Delmonte'.

After Aquakneesha discover she couldn't have me, she then wanted the next thing close in line to me, which was none other than lil Bro Delmonte', see, she had already known how shortcomings didn't actually run in our bloodline, so she knew upfront exactly what she was getting herself into, Ya Dig!

Chapter Eight: Clean Up Woman!

Aquakneesha's a Betty Wright fan calling herself remaking "Clean Up Woman", she's a sanctified Don Julio dranker too, so it's no telling what she'd like to do; she allowed me to know she almost went to see Jesus personally, just by shaving her bikini line, I didn't know if she was throwing slugs, or what?

But she let me know, every time she saw Monte', for some particular reason, her pussy quiver's, even when she met him at the kiosk at the Church; if my Bro wasn't a Deacon, then she'd probably wouldn't even be Saved to this day, she only got baptized because he was supposedly performing her baptism.

I know it may sound pathetic, but Church's nowadays, don't be caring about what or then who's soul they're saving, they just open-handedly welcome you into their congregations; from what I reminisce of, when she and Wifey had gotten in an altercation about some guy, he belonged to another Woman.

It all supposedly started at a gender reveal, Wifey finally lowered her standards, by deciding to get on eHarmony one night, this was before we rekindled, of course; when she was telling me her story, it all sounded so far-fetched, more like a Barnes & Noble novel, if not a plot for a new television soap opera.

Now I had to pay closer attention, I mean I didn't need her knowing exactly what I was thinking about; seriously, if you been paying close attention, then you should automatically know, that winking camel toe, had a lot to do with it, I mean liquor wasn't even involved just yet, well I don't think it was.

She needed some healthy Vitamin Dee, I couldn't help but catch a whiff of her pussy aroma, by me being considered Freaky Dee/Splackavellie; I wasn't gone allow it jeopardize my name/reputation, I clapped twice, you know for my clap-on clap-off effect, I couldn't allow it damper my genes, Ya Dig.

I knew she just being manipulative, but maybe I can fuck her this once, and let her go about her business, it isn't like she has a whip appeal; she isn't Lorena Bobbitt, then again, I hope she isn't because I don't know what I'd do if my dick wasn't attached, he is my King-Ding-a-ling for instance.

Now I know the saying: Teamwork Makes The Dream Work, I guess, Delmonte' forgot I was his Big Bro, and what I say go, I've been reminiscing; I don't know how, I don't know when, but they already plotted to make Love and leave me out their shit, it wasn't right, at all, Hell, I'm the one grieving.

I understand I have a lot on my mind at this time, but right now, I'm the one who been sexually frustrated for these past couple of days, to be honest; as I sit here waiting for Wifey's corpse to finally be prepared for her funeral service, you don't know how many times masturbation has come to mind.

I'm probably the only King Ding-a-ling she knew of, even though we happen to have a funeral we're preparing for; Aquakneesha throwing hints or slugs, not only can she sang, but she'd like to honor her friend with a solo if I didn't mind.

Though she claim to be a nudist, she only gave Bro a peep show.

As she belt out New Home by Olivia Branch Walker a cappella, let's just say it was as if she was auditioning for Sunday Best, and I guess I was none other than Kirk Franklin; she the cause of my eyes getting moist, I mean I already knew her story, I refuse to allow my spirit be gullible, so I held it in.

I'm sure he wouldn't mind Bro digging in his, hell, it ain't like they married, with rumors speculating, she's like a doorknob, everybody get a turn; with me finally becoming a Widower all of a sudden, my conscience don't have to suffer the consequences anymore, she finally get herself a full course of me.

She noticed I'd given her every excuse, well every excuse I could honestly think of, but now Wifey transitioned on to Glory, I know she resting peacefully; seriously, do you think she'd have a problem with me getting close to her so-call bestie, I'm sure she don't want me lonely, no, she belong to lil Bro.

Now, I'm sure you probably heard of the saying, how it's supposedly Bro's Before Hoe's, and I'd go to the end of the earth behind that one there; even though we both have different likes and dislikes, I'll give him the actual shirt off my back if he's ever in need, I wouldn't dare want to see my Bro in need.

I mistakenly saw for myself, Monte' was capable of helping himself out, if you know what I mean, I'm not throwing slugs, because he's more athletic than I am; but we tried our best to cohesively work together, but he got more secrets than I got, well you can take that to the bank, and cash it for yourself.

When the Lord start Blessing, that's when you find out who your real friends are, I mean I never imagine trusting any Women other than Wifey; I can't believe she transitioned to Glory, I'm not Miss Cleo, but I see myself shouting all over the pews, Whatever I do just know my worship is for real!

Chapter Nine: If Only You Knew?

Aqakneesha notice my vulnerability, she let me in on Nesha and her plan, she cried out hysterically, I tried my best to be a gentleman, I held her close to my heart; she was telling me she regret not being her Sis surrogate, it caught me off guard, my mind already born and raised knee deep in the gutter too.

I guess she and Wifey had been discussing having a baby, so I questioned since I knew it was indeed her actual cause of death, I mean I knew it wasn't suicide, I learned she was supposedly a squirter too; well, Delmonte' can't keep secrets for nothing, sure y'all know that's how most little Bro's are anyway.

There I was grieving, or hardly grieving at all, I felt her fingers pinching and squeezing my nipples, it was as if she was trying best to straighten my chest hair surrounding my nipples; I don't have control of my dick at times like this, if we had intercourse, then shouldn't we wait till after the INTERMENT.

I don't know what, or who gave her permission to insert her tongue in my mouth, but for some reason, I started enjoying it to be honest; she began undressing herself, seriously I understood that it's my ego that had me so hyped, but she has me standing in full attention right about now she does, anyhow.

So here I am, sitting on Wifey's toilet, Aquakneesha noticed my dick floating in toilet water, she rush over to start performing cardiopulmonary resuscitation, I wasn't doing any stopping; it was like my dick had gotten a second wind, and started breathing on his own, veins and everything were bulging.

I know it's been said: One Man trash is another Man treasure, I don't recall witnessing Bro sit her out yet, but she came to me at a grieving moment; now I have the slightest idea, of keeping this between us, then again, I'm afraid she may get a little too excited, I'm pretty sure y'all know how that go.

She been consistent about getting a fair taste, I know since I first started courting Wifey, she's been like that third wheel; hold up, now she has the opportunity of having me to herself, I'm more than sure Bro wouldn't mind it, he might even wanna shoot dice for her, money on wood, makes gambling good.

I know I probably shouldn't do him like that, but I'm sure he wouldn't mind, if only he knew what I was talking about, but either way it goes, it's a win-win situation for me; she's always been known as that hoe over there, well now she'd be considered as my hoe over here, Bro suffers from a brain injury.

I know I shouldn't try getting over on him, especially by taking advantage of him like this, I mean it's not like he delusional or something; that's when my phone received a notification from Homies Mortuary informing me, Wife corpse were prepared, I should view her corpse before either service.

Seriously, Wifey is costing me a arm and a leg, Lord know I don't need her reenacting the movie we watched on our date night because that was "If I Can't" on Netflix; since Aquakneesha getting the best of me now, it's a must that I fuck her on my Versace sheets, well that normally goes without saying.

I don't mean to necessarily brag on myself or anything, knowing we come from a family with BIG DICK energy, I can admit Bro and I took after Daddy; I still take after Daddy because I'm still uncircumcised to this day, I'm sure Delmonte' live in regrets now, he denied himself a long time ago.

I know talks probably cheap, I mean, I never left Wifey scorn, that's a lie and the truth ain't in it, maybe I put my job before her, or she notice something about my job she didn't like; I could've thrown her Bedroom Kandi products away, but I'm not insecure, I give her all the Vitamin Dee she need.

Gramp's, was literally the only Man, who gave me not only self-confidence, but also courage, as well as self-esteem to sway around my crib barefooted; I'm very certain you know how Grandpas are or then were, they normally said what they meant, and meant what they normally said, or was that only mine.

Aquakneesha chauffeured Bro and I back to the mortuary, as we arrive back at Homies Mortuary, I'll be honest my body got tensed; as I entered my Brother from another mother dapped me up, before offering me a Brotherly hug, he escorted me to a stretcher holding my Wifey lifeless body in a shroud!

Chapter Ten: Woosah!

I tried my best to put on a front, I tried to hold my composure, I could've acted a plump fool, but then again, a fool is a Man who doesn't believe in God; and he enlighten me, they just pumped my Wife body before embalming her, now what could have possibly transpired, to cause her to commit suicide.

I didn't wanna go off on him, wouldn't that obviously make me look guilty as charged, I see if we experienced domestic violence, she'd be done popped a cap in me; I was pissed at my up-and-coming VISA, because I don't buy shit from no damn Bedroom Kandi, and I'd never order Bullets or a dildo.

"Woosah", let me just calm down, knowing I wouldn't do shit, I vow to Love her in sickness and in health until death do us part; it wasn't a good idea for death to sneak up like this, I mean it snuck up at a time, I didn't even have a side piece, guess it was that thief in the night, I heard so much about.

I need to go ahead vent, you know lay my head on some titties, think about some shit, you know figure this shit out, literally put up with the bullshit; I wonder if Aquakneesha would like to swing by BLOCKBUSTER pick up some flix, for after the funeral, horror I hope, give me an excuse to hold her.

Now I know she notices she's got me feening, or better yet Pussy Whipped as Wifey had me before transitioning, but I gotta hold on till after the funeral; let me go and jack off, see I ain't gone be able to make it until after the funeral, I don't think I can anyways, now she's got me feening for that monkey.

I don't know what she's into, I better start showing some kind of affection or interest by tonight. I know I must get emotional. I need to just set my alarm clock on my iPhone, because I can't just take a quick hoe bath like I use to anymore. Not only would I get sick, but I can't shower and get out like that.

Damn, Damn, Damn, I wonder if Bro gone be too emotional to partake in tonight's festivities, if not I'll be able to handle tonight's shindig on my own; we can do it like we use to, as a matter of fact, I believe that's how we both just so happen to lose our virginity in the first place, we played Hide, Go & Get It.

I don't mind dusting my apron off, I have a strong taste for Stuff Bell Peppers, I'll let Bro shower and eat first so he can get him some sleep; ooh, I'll finally get to eat my dessert, nawl I wouldn't dare try make it look or sound as if I'm Jeffery Dahmer, human flesh isn't tasty, I'm not looking for a victim.

It was just something about her pussy, whenever it got wet, especially while holding on to me, I thought she was trying her best to gossip, but she was sniffing my cologne; who would've ever known Jimmy Choo was what made me so attractive, hold up, that also makes me out to be materialistic?

Now I can't say I don't quite understand, but I don't give a damn what anybody else thinks about me, or even who I'm sleeping with; if it was up to them, I'd probably still be doing me, I'd hate to use R. Kelly as my scenario, but I'd be keeping it on the down low, then again, I wouldn't be exposing myself.

Here I am, knowing Bro nose wasn't stopped up, I can't say he doesn't know pussy aroma, shi-i-it he know more than I'll give him credit for; it isn't like I don't be eavesdropping, rumor has it, he like his Bro, he always check for cornbread fed chicks, he also knows money on wood makes gambling good.

Now you know, it's pathetic, when you must check a monitor, to find out someone's location in your own house, especially when you trying your best to sneak and freak; when I glanced at the monitor, Bro encourages me rather he knows it or not, he's on the patio getting his nut regardless.

I don't mean to act out, but doesn't that mean he don't want to partake in tonight's festivities, I guess he need his strength if he's an active pallbearer tomorrow, right; by me knowing he want to concentrate on laying his Sis In Love down peacefully, I'm sure he don't want to make mistakes.

You see, it's just that kind of energy right there, that only cause me to always want to give him whatever he want, I know I ain't supposed to take him to a gun range; but whenever I happen to go back, then 9xs out of 10, he'd be on my passenger side, hold up, then I'd have to worry about my life.

I'm sure he wouldn't take me out, he wouldn't bring up old shit, well I hope he wouldn't anyway, I always been a Big Bro towards him, I mean I'd fuck a motherfucker up over him; here I am wondering if I ever been heated with him, that's Baby Bro, I mean I help name him Delmonte', let me go to sleep!

Chapter Eleven: It'll All Come Out In The Wash!

Never in a million years, did I think my walls were as gentle as they are. Aquakneesha ask a specific question; she wasn't concerned about anything else, she wanted to know if I qualified. It must be a rhetorical question or something. She waited all these years for a opportunity, now she killing my vibe.

I knew Bro was taking a nap, I offered Aquakneesha my appetizer, she'll get the full course after the interment; she just laid there with both legs gapped apart, she played with her pearl tongue as if my tongue needed direction's, or even a guide, I mean with the aroma, I could find it blindfolded: Ya Dig.

Seriously, I can't say the aroma wasn't familiar, it filled my nostrils up, now any Man know pussy like the best part of waking up, oh my bad, that's Folgers in your cup, isn't it; I'm sure y'all know how I feel about my feet, Aquakneesha waited till my face lowered to slurp her pussy, before rubbing my sock off.

Wifey find some type of excuse or even reason to crack on my feet, Aquakneesha must have a foot fetish or something, because she hasn't insulted them yet; I know she smell the sweat on my feet while sucking each toe separately, one by on, I wasn't interfering or refereeing, it's every Man for himself.

Now I have the slightest idea why she call me Sir, Sir is one of my alter ego's, but I ain't mad at myself, Freaky Dee isn't bad ether; evidently, she wanted me to lie down on my stomach, in more of a push-up position, that's when I couldn't help but noticing her tongue slide deep into the crack of my, Hell-o.

Seriously, I remember Wifey telling me, she thought her friend Aquakneesha was bipolar, I believe our feelings were actually mutual; I wanted to stop her in her tracks, but knowing this heifer hoe, she'd slide one from her actual scalp, I can never be too careful, not when I'm trying best to sneak and freak.

I know Bro, probably wouldn't mind, it isn't as if they have a commitment, I know I should at least respect his space; I hope he isn't eavesdropping through these gentle walls, hell, I mean they wouldn't have known each other if it wasn't for me in the first place, so I think I deserve this opportunity.

Besides she my Wifey's bestie, so me and her were destined to fuck around regardless, isn't that normally how it goes; I mean, I don't like this actual feeling, but I know Aquakneesha didn't like the feeling of being second best, for all these years to finally come, now she's the center of my attention.

Now I can't believe I'm gone say this, but with all of her shenanigans like trying to compare me to my lil Bro, she's gone be well taken care of as of now, you can trust and believe that; I know you must give in order to receive, I wasn't meaning to get my salad tossed last night, but I must return her favor.

From my fond memory, she needed my tongue assistance, so I won't slide these 13 inches in her yet, but she most definitely has me Pussy Whipped once again; I wonder if I could get inside her pussy for a few seconds, Man fuck it, here gose nothing, it isn't too late for me to take a quick hoe bath.

As hard as my dick is, especially with these exposing veins bulging, I pray I don't fall asleep while surfing the Devil Playground; if I accidentally doze off, I pray Jesus takes the wheel, I don't understand why I feel guilty as of now, I need to bury Wifey, maybe I wouldn't feel as guilty as I feel.

Here I am doing exactly what I didn't wanna do, I mean, I couldn't help but notice my foreskin being so thick and slimy looking, it swollen her inner pussy lips; I mean, I couldn't help myself but kiss, and suck both her chocolate areolas, it wasn't like that isn't what she was hoping to provoke me of doing.

I know this isn't only me sensing it, but I got a strong feeling she trying her best, to make me tap out first, I'm sorry because it ain't gone happen, captain; Anesha tried this before herself, hold up, they must've gossiped at her salon, it definitely wouldn't have surprised me, but she's being too aggressive.

I should get up, go hit the shower quickly, maybe I'll call it a night, what y'all think, then again, I'm not as rude as most Men are; I should find out more about her so-called Christian values, nawl then again, I wouldn't even get myself any sleep whatsoever, so let me just get up now, and go take my shower.

As I made it to the bathroom, I couldn't help but noticing, Bro bikini stuffed in a corner, I understood exactly what Wifey meant by It'll All Come Out In The Wash; Bro wear a medium to expose his dick, I guess he thought that's what I did, but I'm glad to know I aspire him to this day: Ya Dig!

Chapter Twelve: Good Morning Wood!

So here I am just now waking up as if a rooster crowed or something. Morning wood normally greets me first in the morning, before I even run into my bathroom full speed in my Birthday suit; here I am standing before my stall, dick still on brick. It startled me when she reached and hug me from behind.

I couldn't help noticing the aroma of breakfast being prepared, Aquakneesha got up early to prepare breakfast before the family car arrived, to escort us over to the funeral; then again, I'd be tired, and sleepy during the funeral, now how'd it look for me to be on the first pew sound asleep while snoring.

Now I knew, Wifey was one of a kind, so I got myself a RED tailor-made suit designed by my lil bro from another mother over at K. L. Bespoke, I'm telling y' all it's gonna be a head turner; I know most couples often dress alike back in high school, but at least Wifey and I still would be Color coordinated.

To the family and friends, they already said they're wearing all shades of RED, since RED's indeed her favorite color, I went ahead bought myself a pair of RED Ray-Ban shades; because I still gotta be fly as I can be, no matter what, you know I gotta be flossing even while I'm inside of the funeral service.

Seriously, I don't mean to say it out loud or anything, but I feel Gramps all in my spirit when I start singing out: "Shine On Me", "Shine On Me", let the light from the lighthouse,

"Shine On Me"; I mean I don't know exactly why I'm wrenching back to those good ol Gospel Hymns, there before my time.

Aquakneesha couldn't help but notice I was completely butterball naked, I mean I believe all Women just so happen Love witnessing all Men physiques; I sort of regret being the actual cause of her distraction, I just regret jacking off earlier, because I can't help but feel sleep trying to approach me.

I saw her standing before that hot stove sweating like a Hebrew slave, damn, now she can't seem to help herself out but start hyperventilating again, especially whenever it came down to me of course; in a way, I wondered, if that's going to be a good thing, or then again if it's going to be a rather bad thing.

Now I know it's going to be a lot of slow singing and flower-bringing, but I still gotta prepare myself to finally be able and ready to release my Queen by let go, by letting God have his way; I mean He's already blessed our union with years of unconditional Love, so I must finally accept what God allows.

Let me go ahead turn my cordless phone ringer off, because I can already sense how my clientele, well damn, I meant my fans about to be calling in after today; I better stop assuming shit before I must eat exactly what I speak of, but then again, don't just about all Men normally have humongous appetites.

I mean, I don't know how long I'll be coping, I already got Aquakneesha next in line to receive her miracles and blessings; with me releasing so much nut earlier this morning, I know for a fact I'm knocking somebodies

Daughter, Sister, Mother or their Grandmother up, what, I don't discriminate.

Now I know I must choose, lose, or be confused, but tonight Aquakneesha can finally light all Wifey candles surrounding this house, look don't knock it until you try it; oh Lord, here she go with those creepy eyes again, if she can lose those and stop creeping me out, I can finally open up my heart to her.

Ladies, Wouldn't you prefer a Man's heart, instead of his mind, any Man can fuck or make Love to you crazy, but it's that specific Man who'd make love to your body, mind, and soul; I understand how talk is supposedly cheap, but I think I need to go on a hiatus for a minute, or meditate for just a second.

Lord, here I am sighing, I mean you didn't even place Wifey under hospice care, you know giving me an opportunity to get myself situated first; ooh, Lord please forgive me, I'm so sorry for thinking of myself first, I know it's obviously said how death come like a thief in the night, here I am just whining.

By my foreskin looking all slimy, I need to go ahead and rub the tip through her puckered up pussy lips, if she's as fertile which as she suppose to be, she'd get pregnant regardless; I know I shouldn't offer her any, because I heard of the Salon gossip about us uncut Brotha's having Turkey dicks.

I informed y'all once before, I was born and raised knee-deep in the gutter, I'm sure y'all already recognize what kind of dreams I often have throughout the night; Jesus please allow death pass over me yet once again Holy Ghost, this I Pray Lord Jesus, I Love You Abundantly and Beyond: AMEN!

Chapter Thirteen: These Mannish Thought's!

Once again, Aquakneesha's up early as if a rooster crowed, I gripped her from the small of her back, I brought her in for a thankful hug "ooh shit", I didn't mean to expose these mannish thoughts, but I know it's disrespectful to put a time limit on anyone remark as of today, Lord have you're way O God.

I feel as if I need to relax, stop thinking about knocking the cobwebs, or dust off her pussy, I understand I started by waking up from a dream earlier; but I'm gone eventually learn how much of a Woman she is, I bet she probably has these exact same thoughts running through her mind about me.

For instance, like how she'd knock the cobwebs or better yet dust off my tankless BLACK Anaconda, it's a good thing if she does think that kind of way in the first place; hopefully, I'm not alone having these kind of mannish thoughts, knowing how Men are supposedly easily influenced by all women.

I guess she finally has more than enough self-confidence to say: Freaky Dee, I'm sorry, you have my condolences, knowing Wifey been deceased longer than 48 hours, that should've been the first thing she mentioned, she enlightened me, she cleaned and reused Wifey's douche, hanging in the shower.

Now, I don't know if she trying to manipulate me, or thought I'd be gullible enough to believe, her pussy is as tight as it once was, that's not even my concern nowadays; still, she got me Pussy Whipped again, I need to go ahead, get myself ready for Wifey funeral, never thought I'd be saying that.

I never imagined losing my own particular Wifey, I mean not with all the sins I committed in my past, I know she was probably more of a Christian than I am; besides I mean, I clearly understand she is, or was older than I am, I guess I better start rethinking about, how I'm gone make all of my money back.

Game Recognize Game, I don't know why I got Players Club in my head, but I can't help reminiscing of: Diamond, Ronnie & Tricks say; Some Of Us Gotta Use What We Got, To Get What We Want, And Stop Messing With This Chump Change, I can't get that out of my head, but I know I need too.

Wifey got on my last nerve, always wanting to up and get new carpet suddenly. Seriously, I mean, I didn't even know if she was just being funny, or if she was cracking on my bare feet and or toes; all I ask of you, savior, is for you to Create in me a clean heart, and renew in me the right spirit, O God.

I know it's probably normal, I act this kind of way as of now anyhow, but I'm still trying my best to Accept What God Allows, and cope with the situation; Lord, right now I wish I could listen to Twinkie Clark, I know I just need to meditate, to be absent from the body, is to be present with the Lord.

You got people dropping cakes and pies off, for instance, like Mother Boyd from the Sanctuary Missionary Baptist Church; I mean I don't trust all Women, for instance, like those young Mother's may try using Ex-lax, nawl that sound more like Mother Boyd, I should mostly be concerned about.

Instead of cases of 12-packs, you can tell some of these young Mothers has gotten their food stamps, because my kitchen counter, can pass for an actual convenience store; I mean I got cases of 24, 36, I even got bottles of mini juices as well as water, whoever got these Beer's, Thanks but no Thank You.

Now that I'm a Man, and now that I'm able to drive across the bridge to purchase my own, I don't even have a taste for anybodies type of beer; now liquor is a completely different story, Wifey even warned me I needed to stop drinking so much, or she'd up and leave me to myself, O-M-G, that's what she did.

It's me, it's me, it's me O Lord, requiring Prayer, I know sometimes I think of myself, and be considered as my own worst enemy, but Lord I know I shouldn't be having an anxiety or panic attack right now, here KB is texting to inform me, that he was assigned to drive the family car for us today.

He'll get to see me bust out in one of his originals, and hopefully, I'll make him proud by wearing his suit, Lord, just look at the time, so I yell out in my deep Barry White bass-baritone voice; I just pray that everyone riding in this family car is ready, KB just texted me, he's on his way over here now.

Wait a minute, it's only 3 of us, so we'd do better driving my car instead, here we all go looking just as good as we wanna look; yawl come on here he is now, I swung open the door, we run to the Homies Mortuary Funeral stretch limo, it's only three of us, so I hope we aren't the laugh of the Funeral!

Chapter Fourteen: A Virtuous Woman!

I'm glad we pull up to The Sanctuary Missionary Baptist Church in the family car, because the parking lot was overcrowded, to be honest, doesn't this cause you to wonder how it'd be if it was yours; I don't want to jeopardize my own life, I can't argue with God for calling when he get's good and ready too.

Here we are finally exiting the limousine, lining up to get in a single file line, I noticed KB was scoping me out, and saw how I rocked my RED Timbs, with his RED suit; now you can tell how the attire for the funeral was meant to be, which is casual as usual, you can tell I definitely wanted to stand out.

You can tell, I'm a trendsetter because watch just how all Men are gone start dressing for their Wife funeral, matter of fact, let me just shut my mouth; before I accidentally help them over at Homie's Mortuary, because if they receive anymore corpse, shouldn't I too be getting paid for word of mouth.

 Now I know this wasn't my fantasy, then again I can't see myself being without my Wifey, it's a good thing I already know: To Be Absent From The Body, Is To Be Present With The Lord; if she gone home to be with Jesus, then I most definitely won't complain, besides she belonged to him first anyways.

Here we are loading up, all I hear is Aquakneesha sobbing, I wanted to turn around and slap nothing but the living fire out of her, then again wouldn't that be considered an assault;

I mean it wasn't even seconds ago, she was singing: Pound Town, now her face is all flooded in these here unnecessary tears.

I lower my RED Ray-Ban shades, before licking my upper lip, gently sucking my bottom Lip, now you can't tell me I don't know how to flirt; now she got my bladder going, I mean I wasn't planning on going to the bathroom, well definitely not until after my Wifey's burial vault is closed and even sealed.

Lord, I pray that check, deposited in my Bank Account, because I can leave here, and head straight to the BMW dealership, I know my future RED SUV is just waiting for me; now I know for a fact, I said that I wasn't even concerned about my Wifey's life insurance policy, but don't every little bit count.

I also know: Cleanliness is next to Godliness, so Anesha; baby girl, I still Love You with all of my heart, may you finally rest in perfect peace Sweetie Pie, oh Lord, here come those random tears; I mean I can feel em about to start running down my cheeks right about now, they're all up in the webs of my eyes.

Order of Service

The Sanctuary Missionary Baptist Church

Officiating: Bishop Ramzel O. Williams

Reverend H. L. Thomas

11:00 AM

PROCESSIONAL

"Walk In The Light"

CONGREGATIONAL SONG

"Shine On Me" Let The Light From The Lighthouse, "Shine On Me"

SCRIPTURE READING

Old Testament

Pastor Carlton Scott

New Testament

Elder Calvin Coolidge Robertson Jr.

PRAYER

Min. Brandi Hall

SPECIAL SOLO TRIBUTE

Aquakneesha Jefferson: There's A Story Behind My Praise

CHURCH RESOLUTIONS

The Sanctuary Missionary Baptist Church

CHOIR

Can God/God Can!

Da Blessin's Gospel Choir

SPECIAL REMARKS

CHOIR

I Am A Witness

Da Blessin's Gospel Choir

EULOGY

Reverend Kyle Dixon: Freaky Dee

SPECIAL REMARKS/RECESSIONAL

Special Solo

STORMY: I Won't Complain

PARTING VIEW

Homies Mortuary

Da Blessin's Gospel Choir

Let The Church Say Amen

Laurel Land Cemetery

6000 South R. L. Thornton Freeway (Interstate 35)

Dallas, Texas 75232 United States!

Chapter Fifteen: Ashes Too Ashes

So we're all sobbing after just exiting Homies Mortuary stretch limo, I don't understand what could've transpired with Bro today; I mean not only did he go to bed early just last night, but his clumsiness as of today, it reminds me so much of Steve Urkel in a way, he always snort before asking Did-I-Do-That.

You'd think jacking off on the patio, took his strength away as of today, but he usually lift barbells daily, so I had the slightest idea what transpired; he took it HARD, but I may had taken it worst, well Aquakneesha had moments, we all broke down eventually, but we finally released those white doves.

I don't wanna attend the repast, I got all that food back at the house, Aquakneesha chimed in by saying we can warm the bread pudding, and food's everyone been dropping off; we can barbecue those Corn On The Cob's, Lamb Chops, Aquakneesha, you know how to make Baked Beans & Potato Salad?

Delmonte', began laughing hysterically, as if he's Sofia off The Color Purple, that's when suddenly, I couldn't help myself but say: I guess The Dead Has Risen; though we were hurting, we definitely needed that laugh, we already been crying all day, that was the laugh that would keep us from crying.

You know it's pathetic, how my mind still live knee-deep in the gutter or deeper in sin, I was just reminiscing about all 3 of us back in the days; I mean you couldn't miss us sneaking off to play Hide Go & Get It, but that was way back in all of our pre-Cumming days, and I hope we weren't alone.

I gave Aquakneesha the side eye, she gave Delmonte' the side eye, he look back to me smizing. he and I both said: "Clock It", in unison, that's when we burst out laughing; DAMN-DAMN-DAMN, I need to run to my car, grab those condoms out my glove compartment, because we ain't playing no games.

I know some people may not be able to understand me at this point, but one thing I most definitely admit to is God created 2 Men when he Blessed our Mama with us; there isn't anything wrong with my Bro & I reminiscing about our yesteryears, hold up, I think she's about ready for this manajatwa again.

Let me light each candle, surrounding this house. I'm so tired of grieving. I can place a smile back on Aquakneesha's face yet once again; it won't necessarily be the exact same, but hopefully, it'll at least brighten up her mourning feeling. Now Bro has a decision to make, whether he's in or ether he's out.

So, I turn it on Marvin Sease Pandora station on my iPhone, he quickly reminded me I could be a "Motel Lover"; if I were going to take all Wifey pictures down all over, her memory would still be installed in my conscience, I continue hearing her say: I KNEW YALL HAD SOMETHING GOING ON.

I wouldn't care if Wifey is mad at me right now, I would do or give anything just to hear my Wifey's voice, at least one more time; that's it, my Wifey just mentioned: I was supposed to only have her DICKMATIZED, and obsessed as well, I should've known that HOE was trying to steal my Husband.

Damn-Damn-Damn, I don't know why I feel so nervous, I know Wifey expect me to present the Best Man I could be; shouldn't I walk her out to her car, I mean I noticed that I don't even have on any socks, or any shoes whatsoever, and I haven't heard anyone cracking on my feet, say in about a week.

For some particular reason, Bro doesn't want to be affiliated with Aquakneesha, he probably came to his senses at the funeral; I'm pretty sure he grieving because I know everybody grieves differently, so I know if he flipping out with Aquakneesha now, if I'm not mistaken, I'm probably up next.

I haven't brush my teeth, gargled, or washed my face yet, and Aquakneesha hasn't even tried coming for me; I wonder if by her preparing breakfast was either a routine, or if it was rather a scheme, I mean she already knew everything else, maybe she just trying her best to be generous, all of a sudden.

You know isn't it crazy, when you can't find your own socks, or shoes the following morning, so I don't know if she put it on us, or what; Bro already don't like talking, so you know it must be something, because not one time had he stuttered or anything, he quickly said: We Gotta Get Her Out.

Now I don't know if this is the beginning of our partnership, or if this is just our Brotherly Bond/Love, but one thing I just so happen to know is that can't nobody separate us anymore, Ya Dig; so, from ashes to ashes, dust to dust, you're still my Baby Brother, so not even Pussy can separate us: Ya Dig!

Chapter Sixteen: Corporation!

Here I am, just pulling off from this BMW dealership, Aquakneesha following behind me in my Black-on-Black BMW which as I had before Wifey transitioned; I mean she always talk about buying some RED BMW SUV, I know I shouldn't reminisce on the past, I just knew she liked showing off.

With Anesha, I had to fulfill her dreams, Aquakneesha, I have to make her dreams into a reality: Ya Dig; now I know Anesha was probably afraid of losing me too Aquakneesha, because she wasn't able to bear my child on her own, I told her we could even adopt, but I guess it wasn't good enough for her.

I guess if she couldn't have my child her own, she didn't want to witness anyone who could, that's probably why she had me assuming Aquakneesha was a DUDE; Aquakneesha tried best explaining, she was supposedly tomboyish all her life, that's why she had me saying we're not judgmental.

I mean, I knew I should merge off this freeway, go confess this surprising undying Love I found in Aquakneesha, but she already been through my family; I know it's been myself, and my Bro Monte', but hell, if we already been up and through her valley, then I'm pretty sure there's others who's leaped.

Every year, our Family Reunion exposes our deepest skeletons, so to be honest, we have trophies made up for the grand prize winner. I suppose you could say Harry Hines Blvd. is literally our stomping ground. G-G knew us before we knew ourself; she knew that we were always up to no good.

When you got hustling in ya genes, maybe I need to run my fits by the cleaners, Ya Dig, you know I'm feeling myself right about now, I want to be seen and not viewed; I need to stop by the crib, scoop Aquakneesha, hopefully, Bro isn't home, if he is, he's in for a rude awakening, today he is anyway.

These have to be those secrets, most Bros kept from each other, but as for me and my lil Bro, we aren't much concerned or even worried about this chick; if Bro get to her before I do, then so be it, he knows how to clean up after himself, because he already knows how, Momma didn't raise no fool, Ya Dig.

I'm glad I don't have to worry about any animosity with him, Bro wouldn't dare want to ever duke it out over no pussy, that's not even in our bloodline; we refuse to allow some chicken head, come in between our Brotherly bond, we weren't even brought up foolish like that, so you can literally miss us.

Now I'd apologize for overstepping my boundary, we aren't about to scrap over no pussy, I guess Daddy could literally see our future in our past, no wonder why he chastised us before transitioning; I guess, he already recognize what a whiff of pussy aroma does for his youngest son, of course.

By the way, she been magnetically stuck to us throughout the years, I don't know why, but I have a feeling she'll try impregnating herself using a turkey baster; I better warn lil Bro about tapping out early, even if it's accidental, I hope she isn't on her menstrual cycle, because now I'm even feening.

Instead of my normal hoochie daddy shorts, I normally parade around my crib in, I was trying my best to be polite, so I put my night pants on, and hell, they didn't do any better; seriously you can't help but recognize my humongous bulge saluting, now at least I do try my best, keeping my dick on a leash.

You see, it isn't my fault he acts like an untamed gorilla, whenever and wherever I decide to go, he always tries to represent where he's from, just because he's from Dallas; Oak Cliff, that's his hood, he's been known to put it in your face, and get that shit understood, see what I mean, at times he is ratchet.

Others say that he only suffers from a narcissistic personality, I believe that only comes from his being antisocial for so long; now I wasn't going to continue stripping, well I was at first, but then Anesha was just about tired of everyone else getting a total glimpse of her main dish, before she was even served.

Here I am reminiscing about Anesha, she was telling me her salon's gossip, like how Aquakneesha start experiencing hot flashes; hold up, how in hell could she suffer it if she a Man, Men don't suffer that time of the month drama, we just know how to ease out Women way during that timing.

I guess Anesha had known how gullible I was, before hearing the sounding of that great and mighty trumpet; now Father, I Pray I make it to Heaven one of these days, but if she's in hell due to her lying habits, she's all alone because not even I would like to experience that heat!

Chapter Seventeen: Choose, Lose or be Confused!

Now, I know the Bible say: Judge Not That Ye Be Not Judged, by me finally being head Pastor of the Sanctuary Missionary Baptist Church, that goes for me as well; hopefully, it doesn't offend the majority of my choir members as of now anyhow, like for instance those sopranos, Altos or Tenors.

See Gramps never told me before transitioning to Glory, nearly all the choir members were Monogamous, that isn't for me to be concerned about, now is it; we all got to receive that surprising wakeup call, on that getting up morning, so I can't fend for you, well neither can you fend for me.

Our goal is to make it to Heaven, I'm pretty sure y'all know into eternity, where there's no such thing as death, but I can't make anyone else believe what no one has ever witnessed for themselves; I mean we've all experienced dreams once before I'm sure, I heard it through the grapevine for myself also.

Supposedly, Gramps could hear me right now, In that case, I'd gladly like to say Thank You, Gramps, for training me up in the way I should go, so now I'm older, I still haven't departed from it; now I'm sure that y' all see, I try my best to stay on the straight and narrow path, but I sure miss that cash flow.

Anesha enjoyed being pampered or rather spoiled, I mean she could've been spending her own coins, but I'm the breadwinner of my household, so I chose to keep her spoiled rotten; outsiders looked at us as if we were splurging from the Church, but she's my Wifey, so I had the rights to keep her spoiled.

She had so much wardrobe she couldn't take with her, it's to late for me to try and dispute it, I'm gone see if Aquakneesha want any of her possessions; I mean if they were friends like I thought, Aquakneesha should want to cherish all her friend memories, including her Balenciaga boots.

Dang, I mean I can't believe it, I'm thinking about giving up my drinking and smoking, my Doctor just has to find a different route, or routine for me to be medicated; I need to get back into Church, because I guess I been ducking & dodging Church function's so long, that I'm barely recognizable.

I mean, she can finally take Wifey's Victoria Secret and Bedroom Kandi nonsense. As a matter of fact, I'll allow her to make her own decision, because if she chooses to accept my Wifey's interruptions, then she wouldn't have time for me anyways. That's probably why Bro don't want to deal with her.

See, I know I should be concentrating on Church, instead of having myself a pity party, I'm a Man of God, ooh that even sound perverted; I guess because isn't that normally how all those so-call molesting priests would have normally said, I know it's to get themselves out of trouble, I'm sure of.

I'm sure y' all know, I don't need or better yet want Aquakneesha as my pond, if that's what she assume I need her company for, she has another thing coming; I only suffer the consequences of keeping her company, keep her awake behind the steering wheel, I don't need that on my conscience.

I know how God works in mysterious ways and all, but here I am just wondering why my Gramps didn't leave his Church towards my Bro, I mean he has the faith the size of a mustard seed as well; neither one of us has a family just yet, and by his narcolepsy, he'd probably be the first between us.

Although I'm the oldest, I should've been done sowing wild oats by now, I'm not afraid but you have to focus on things such as S.T.D's; if you Love yourself the same as I Love myself, you'd probably be my very next-door neighbor, I'm not trying to cap on anyone, especially when I know it could've been me.

Had the Lord not sat me down, when he did, I'd be considered a addict or dealer then again maybe suicidal, in the worst way; but oh how I Thank God, for saving a wretch like me, now had Gramps not opened up his pulpit to me when he did, I'd probably still be just a nobody, trying to tell everybody.

Ooh wee, I thank God for making a positive change in my life, I mean if I had ten thousand tongues, I still wouldn't be able to tell the Lord Thank You enough; I Thank God for Bishop Richard "Mr. Clean" White & Twinkie Clark because they both taught me just how to finally: "Accept What God Allows".

Even though I'm releasing my Wifey for good, this is More Than I Can Bear, so for me to be happy with or without Anesha, here goes nothing; Lord, I know I Can Do All Things Through Christ Which Strengthens Me, am I being greedy for asking for a rush delivery, for another Woman designed for me!

Chapter Eighteen: Jezebel Spirit!

I don't know why I can't get it out of my head, Aquakneesha gyrated and rode me as if I was a mechanical bull, now my temptation can't be stopped, I know for a fact she the one alright; Anesha was quite different, instead of her being the one, she was more like The One God Chose For Me.

Since I knew, we're only meant towards each other for a season, God has to shower on me yet once again, and hopefully, God wouldn't send me any Jezebel Spirit, oops I meant Aquakneesha, or then again would he; I know God has a jokingly side of him, because I was definitely created in his image.

I believe that's exactly where we all just so happen to get our hysterical ways from, because I'm more than a conquer, to know all things work together for the good of the Lord; I know I may have recently made a swift change in my life, but the one thing I Love about God, is that He's an Instant God.

God made a swift change in my life, I mean, long before I was created, He already given me the exact words to speak to myself, during this specific storm raging in my life anyway; when I began to notice her deteriorating, I didn't want to admit it, but I knew death was coming, I just didn't know when.

I'm glad, it finally influenced me to just keep the faith, I know this isn't me talking, but I'm more than prepared for whatsoever God has in store for me next; I mean I can't be afraid of myself, because I am my very own enemy, and I recognize Aquakneesha's the one who's up next, so I need to stop running.

Now, had Daddy still been here, I reminisce of him telling us before, he wasn't even worried about me and June-bug, calling him old anymore, because OLD stands for Out Living Dummies; I mean, I didn't think my Daddy would ever come for his sons like that, but he just kept us on our toes, I guess?

But that was when I first learned about God being such an Instant God, I Prayed for God to instantly heal my Daddy, whether it was here on earth, or up in Heaven, Lord, did I speak death on my own Daddy; it's like I never wanted to sit and watch anyone suffer, that wasn't like me, no way, no how.

I know all is forgiven, so I don't hold any grudges, least Daddy would pick me up when I was a young buck coming up; I never quite understood how important it was for us to spend quality time together, as much as we possibly can, I look at myself and I can't help but recognize Daddy, all up in my face.

See, I know it's that Instant God who's using my past experience, to brighten either my destiny or should I say my even brighter future; I know God has been known for doing all things well, so maybe I should at least check into my past, see if I have any illegitimate children, since way back when.

Lord, I know what goes around obviously comes around, these last couple of days turn out to be some of the best days of my life; I mean I don't know what to expect of them, but I wonder exactly what happened to both my estranged cousins from 44 Acres Homes, down in the Houston area.

Now honestly, I don't know why I'm so worried about others right about now anyhow, had Nesha been either one of their Wives, then I'd most definitely would've been there for each of their support; I just can't believe this one here at all, we'd both come down to Houston, Anesha would always cook for us.

Am I overreacting, I know for a fact, something must've transpired because I know they wouldn't have left me hanging, out of all people, this isn't like them; they the main ones saying blood is supposedly thicker than water, they wouldn't even answer their phone, well maybe they didn't have a signal.

Maybe I need to take a quick nap or something, you know calm down and relax or something, I already promise myself I wouldn't ever go back to smoking blacks, cigarettes, or weed; but right now, I need to sample me some "Ohh Wee", I'm sure I wouldn't be the only Pastor dranking and or smoking.

I be God dog on it, I might need to go visit my Aunt Mable or Aunt Betty, whosoever I choose to visit, I'm sure they'd get me right; I tried my best to stay prayed up, but I guess Satan was determined to take over my soul either way it goes, Yolanda Adams reminds me, this battle isn't mine, it's the Lord's.

Lord, now I don't know what this actual feeling is that I'm feeling right about now, but Jesus keep your right hand of protection not only covering over me, but my entire family as well; if by any chance you happen to find my little cousin's, please holy ghost direct them right this way, this I pray: AMEN!

Chapter Nineteen: Hay Is For Horses!

Had there not been any cameras still attached to my house, I probably wouldn't have known my cousins from Acres Homes where here; I didn't notice anyone at the funeral, maybe had they spoke, then maybe I would've known, they both said Hey, and I respond by simply saying Hay is for horses.

They recognize I was grieving, DJ reach out offering me some WHITE Reese's as usual, and a compassionate hug, J. Mike notice I'd been crying every since the funeral, he saw I was slightly passing out; he ask DJ to help escort me in. I didn't want to go in, but I need to get off my feet.

I wasn't trying to shed any tears, so to keep from crying, I ask if they want to shoot pool, I mean, I don't keep up with beers, but I got bookoo's of Don over at the bar; eventually, that's what they'd been waiting for, J. Mike then said hold up Bro, let me just gone Bless ya Bro, in his deep southern accent.

Just for me hearing him say those actual words, I mean I ain't gone lie, that was beyond a Blessing, this dude pull out his iPhone, tap in it, my Cash App notification said "DING"; I reach in my pocket, pulled out my iPhone, check my Cash App, and he instantly Blessed me with a thousand dollars.

Ooh, Lord knows, I've never been so gullible before, but all of a sudden there go that damn numb feeling, all in my feet again, I wasn't trying to sound or look as if I was challenged or anything; but I accidentally said it loudly, I sure hope y'all know my Cash App, doesn't believe in giving any of refund.

J. Mike said: he isn't an Indian giver anymore, that aught ta tell ya I been Blessed, to give you a seed Big Bro, DJ overheard, I guess that caused him to get suspicious; it wasn't as if he didn't already hear that "DINGING" sound of my notification go off, he already knew he'd try his best to out due J. Mike.

Not one time, did I mention how much he dropped, but obviously, DJ already knew for a fact it had to be a band; DJ already wore a shady cricked smize plastered on his face, I knew he always like high siding, even when we were young bucks coming up, I knew he couldn't drop more than J. Mike did.

I heard my notification sounding go off again, I wasn't trying to sound or speak high pitched, as if I was experiencing puberty again; but my voice had got real high-pitched and squeaky, DJ then dropped me 2 bands out of suspicion, and hell, that's when I just knew I needed much more than just a drank.

Obviously, these visiting cousins of mine, I don't know what they're calling themselves doing, but if they don't remember, Big Cousin doesn't believe in giving any refunds; like what do they think I do for a living, I know I'm a Pastor and all, but one thing I'm most definitely not, is like our late Gramps was.

I'm pretty sure, when this Church got started, I probably wasn't even thought of just yet, I wish I had a son or a daughter to leave it too; I wonder if I continued to strip on the low, would those messy Church folk still assume I'm still splurging from the Church, they already know I'm a well-dressed Man as is.

So, I don't mean to sound as if I'm arrogant or anything, but holding on to 3 bands like this, I mean I can get myself a gold grill, I may even get myself a little lipo; but why do I hear my conscience trying to mawk Twinkie by singing "Accept What God Allows", maybe it's just God trying to tell me something.

Whenever money is around, for some odd reason Aquakneesha just magically appears out of no wear, as if she the black I Dream Of Jeannie; if she's looking for a quick come-up, no ma'am/no sir I wouldn't dare put her off on my cousins like that, I don't even know if Delmonte' through with her yet.

There she go batting her flirtatious eyes, I can't say she don't know how to flirt or come up with some kind of scheme. She know exactly what her hypnotizing aroma does to Men, Women too: I just don't know, because Wifey was on her as if she was hooked on phonics, and well that's just to be honest.

It's as if she just trying her best to expose herself to me or something, maybe I should finally go ahead allow her to be herself for a change, I know it'll all come out sooner or later; I'm afraid that it's just something I may not want to know about, because I'm still wondering about Wifey's mysterious death.

Aquakneesha went ahead informing me, this guy she & Anesha met off eHarmony, he'd been passing HIV around, she happens to be one's; I mean I knew I wasn't gullible, then again it made too much sense, to be honest, I just wish the funeral home would've opened up to me, and been more honest!

Chapter Twenty: Leave Me Be!

Learning there was a strong possibility, HIV the leading cause of Wifey demise, no offense but I'm glad I don't have symptoms of it myself; I'm feeling fine knowing it wasn't passed to or from me, I can keep living my life, I'd have to find myself another WIFEY, and Church will no longer be my option.

I don't want to have anything else to do with Aquakneesha, if Wifey's leading cause of death was HIV, which as it was suppose to had been, why hasn't Aquakneesha contracted it herself; I don't know why she hasn't dropped dead, I don't think I want it surrounding me, all up in my face taking up my space.

Even though I wish Aquakneesha would leave me be, I can finally hear her out this last time, I know she always need water whenever she come around; she informed me she's been taking PrEP, along with her birth control, since graduating High School, Anesha's the one saying how she wasn't a lab rat.

She always said how she'd rather be seen and not viewed, now it's too late to even try mentioning that, because just by us glancing at her corpse, it tore us all up as of today anyway; I guess you could say was also when Aquakneesha began dry snitching, telling me I didn't know my own Wife's fetishes.

Now, I didn't want to let her know she was right all alone, but seriously I didn't know Wifey had any fetishes, I mean, I didn't even know that much for myself; Aquakneesha mentioned Wifey assumed I'd been cheating on her, because of my underwear, what I'm trying to say is farts come naturally, Ya Dig.

Last I knew, Wifey had an upper respiratory infection, so that's exactly what I'm believing as well as knowing was the main cause of her demise; I mean Wifey, didn't want me stripping anymore, so I answered my full-fledged calling back into the pulpit, it's way more than just me who's a backslider.

I know the word says: He who is without sin amongst you shall cast the first stone, that alone enlightens me I'm not standing alone: now I'm not trying to expose anyone, but I remember Gramps telling me before transitioning on to Glory, No Man Is Perfect, which is why we must repent on a daily.

And I know there's a hand-full, if not majority of so-call Christian Communities who's been so quick to judge or point their finger at the person next to them; now I mean, I can't say that I'm the one to blame, but what I don't want is to get myself all caught up in something that I can't get myself out of.

I need to stop stressing myself, before I end up buried in a grave right next to her, I know her death was unexpected, so I should leave it at that; I don't know why I want to blame myself suddenly for her untimely demise, I am innocent until proven guilty, and that's not only by the court of law: Ya Dig?

Seriously, I know for a fact I miss our cuddling sessions, I knew Love was supposedly a gamble, kissing was supposedly a game; but now that I can finally admit to it, my Wifey's transitioning is much more than just a pain, I know everyone may grieve differently, and this isn't just me I'm talking too.

My Lord, how can I quickly get over Wifey's unexpected demise, Jesus you know, I don't like the actual feeling of being lonely, I don't think anyone do to be honest; so here I am trying my best to meditate, "I Won't Complain" just will not leave my thought process, I know God is with me always.

He already made it perfectly known, when He promised He'd never leave me, nor forsake me, even I know His word is still instilled, up in my head as well as still in my heart, to this actual day anyway; my late Gramp's sermon title was "I-I-I Know He's Alright", he said it was from genesis to revelations.

I'll never forget those Sunday School classes back then; I remember having Sis. Carson, & Sis. Burks as my Sunday School teacher's; ooh not only do I miss my Wifey very badly, but I also miss those 2 essential souls as well, you know at times, I remember those good ol days that, we all used to have.

Now, what I believe I need to do is look up HOMEAGLOW on the Internet, because I'm not trying to sound conceded or anything; but I can't sleep inside of a hovel, I've never been known as a nasty kind of person, and I never will for as long as I shall live, I mean that doesn't even meet my quota, Ya Dig.

I never been considered a hoarder, so I need to go ahead and start cleaning this house because I've never witnessed any spiderwebs before Wifey transitioned; now she's gone, I have to clearly understand she's not just running to the corner store or anything, she's moved to A Brand-New Life!

Chapter Twenty-One: Back To Normalcy!

Now, it wasn't long before I began recognizing I was cleaning my very own crib, with God's help, of course, Jesus is someone I can't make it without; I guess you can say I'm getting back to normalcy because Gramps and Grantee' reared Monte' and I up, to make it with or without a Wife by our side's.

I don't know if J. Mike and DJ where both high as a skunk, before taking a cat nap from their road trip or whatnot, but I wasn't lying about their refunds; I'm just glad I set up an online bank account, I can trust and believe everything been deposited, I'm not gone act like I didn't think this wasn't bad money.

They both woke up with the major munchies, as if they got high before they arrived here or something, but then again, I guess that's normally how all weed heads are regardless; not once had either of them ask about their money or anything; they asked if I knew were they could treat me to some fresh tilapia.

I don't know why I'm acting so paranoid all of a sudden. I often wonder if they both forgot how they had already Blessed me far beyond my beliefs, but seriously, I don't recall picking a restaurant yet; I know how they may even consider moving here, especially after they've both eaten over at Nana B's.

Now every time we in the Houston metroplex, it's a must we stop by Shipley's Doughnuts 6602 N. Shepard Houston Texas 77091, I think those are the best; but there I go letting y' all know something y' all probably didn't know anything about in the first place, all of this free advertising that I'm doing.

We about to go out in public, so let me throw on this new Jordan jogging suit on, my brand-new J's Delmonte' hooked me up with; ooh wee, there I go snitching, I better be careful I hope whosoever reading this piece of work, isn't affiliated, because even the Lord knows I'm too old to fight anymore.

Let me just do my early morning routine: brush my teeth, gargle, floss, wash my face, do 100 push-ups. Man, let me go ahead get ready, stop trying my best to waste time. I mean, I know that bullets don't have anybody's name on them, but I think I'm just nervous about riding along with them.

I know I shouldn't assume the worst or anything, but wasn't I the one who was upset about Wifey assuming the worst for me; either way it go, I'm going to have to put my trust back in the Lord, and that'll be every day of my life, I think it was by me hearing HIV, is literally what really frightened me.

Okay, I don't know, if HIV was the leading cause of Wifey demise, then shouldn't I have it as well, doctors probably just hasn't seen mine for themselves, doesn't that make any sense to y'all; I know by going out to eat with family, this probably my last meal before hearing that trumpet sound for myself.

At times, it's like I'm okay with dying, but I think of everything I'd be leaving behind, I know that Heaven is my goal each & every day; I mean I don't know how the devil even became friends with my conscience, because I don't be thinking about weed like I use to anymore, but since y' all brought it up.

That's because I'm a Man of the cloth, I try my best not to interfere with my old tendencies or old ways anymore; I need to drive my new car, meaning it's a no-smoking zone, hopefully, they'll understand I'm no longer about that life anymore, ever since I've given up sin, hallelujah, I been born again.

Maybe I should see this as my farewell ride, well other than in that hearse escorting me over to the Church, last but not least over to my gravesite; honestly, God know me and my heart better than I do, and better than I know of myself, this remind me of the bug I just had not so long ago, so I'm Gucci.

J. Mike ran in my master bathroom, DJ ran inside the bathroom on down the hallway, now I wanted to be messy, but I just couldn't see myself entertaining the devil, not like that anyway; I know the devil comes to steal, kill, and to destroy, but God came so that I may have life, and life more abundantly.

Now here I am Big Cousin and all, I had a couple extra pairs of hoochie daddy shorts, well they were going to waste anyway, I asked if they need them to ride home in; I'm just glad they couldn't read my mind at that specific timing anyhow, but they quickly got my picture and raised up off my couch.

I didn't want to offer any goodbye hug's, I just had to make it seem as if I was expecting an actual hug from each of them; if only you knew what I was praying to myself as they were departing my house, I prayed they made it back home safely, and I immediately hit the shower, we'll reunite at the reunion!

Chapter Twenty-Two: Welfare Check!

They couldn't seem to find any signal here, now all of a sudden they leave my house calling to do a Welfare Check upon me; I know they don't Love me that much, not to be checking upon me every couple of miles, because I know they couldn't have gotten far, I mean there isn't no way possible.

Then again, those my BLOOD cousins on my Momma side, well I'm pretty sure they feel like they have a need too speed as well; see, that part of my actual family doesn't believe in any kinds of road rage at all, and if you do anything to interrupt their sanity, you'd just have to pull over and duke it out; Ya Dig.

Now I don't purposely mean to expose our truths or anything, but if you look up community dick in the dictionary, no offense or whatnot, but you'd probably find each of us posted up at Grantee's crib; all women know, the quickest way to a Man heart is too feed his stomach, but Wifey couldn't cook.

That's probably one of the only reason's, I really couldn't call my card in stolen, because Wifey and I stayed going out to eat, at least every Sunday anyways; I mean they'd literally argue me up and down saying how it's coincidental, I have several repeated charges from places, which I deny ever going too.

I don't have to rob Peter in order to pay Paul, I need to quit acting bougie, because I know I'm finally doing better as of now anyhow; preaching the word of God isn't just my true calling, it most defiantly isn't considered my side hustle, see, I Luh God, You Don't Luh God, What's Wrong With Chu?

I was so grateful for even having the opportunity of meeting up with Erica, as well as Tina Campbell or should I just say MARYMARY; I mean they honestly don't even know just how much their music help's me too meditate on a daily, you see I knew I wasn't exactly what my Wifey called a sexaholic.

O God Yes, I honestly think I'm ready to finally admit to myself, I'm seriously in need of Grief Counseling, I know I probably should've been in some type of Counseling before Wifey transitioned; then again I believe there's no time, other than the right time, which is right now anyhow, so Woosah.

Wifey isn't even present on this side anymore, not too surprise me with a Dirty 30th shindig, I may as well try my best to surprise myself; I wonder why God uses my self conscience all of a sudden anyway, I think, I know the difference between the voices, why am I reminiscing about Aquakneesha suddenly.

Maybe God is finally so quick to remind me of each of my flaws and or mistakes, and well I know the right thing to do is to apologize, but she may not even forgive me, well probably not for this time she won't; well I know I can't use any type of reverse psychology on her, Lord, wouldn't I be in the wrong.

I'm sure I literally killed any relationship we could've ever had, I know I shouldn't have wished death upon that living vessel of God; you see I know the potter wants to put me back together again, honestly the potter's been putting me back together, since I was yea high too a grasshopper.

Now I can't say wishing death on someone isn't a sin, I know when I go to the Father for myself, I got some serious explaining to do; we Preachers also sin, just like the very next Man does, we too must beg and plead for forgiveness, because there's no Sin greater than the next, God don't show favoritism.

I can't keep sugarcoating my very own wrong doing, in fact let me just call her up right now, hopefully she answers my phone call; because I just don't need her assuming I only wanted her because she was my Wifey's bff, but I should remember that so-called HIV status, because she's probably up next.

Knowing I shouldn't judge a book by it's cover, I really just don't know how, but there's something I can't even seem to let go of about her, and she just one of them; I mean I don't know if it was because of her naughty pillow talking or whatnot, but I think I even Love her soft whispers off up in my ear.

Honestly, I mean can't no Man deny himself of being aroused by any particular Woman whispering sweet nothings in his earlobe; I know I shouldn't be assuming or wishing anything, well I know that's probably a dream deferred to be honest, so maybe I should just keep my head, from out of the clouds.

But I know won't nothing ever transpire, if I don't ever Man up and stop being so freaking nervous, especially about what outsiders looking in think or even say; seriously I can only be one Man, and I know God is literally my one and only judge, He's who I have to worry about getting sentenced by!

Chapter Twenty-Three: I Am Not Ashamed!

Jesus, whatsoever I may be doing in you're sight Jehovah, please allow it to be acceptable towards you Father, PLEASE Guide Me O God: I'm not trying to say I'm perfect in any kinds of way, but I'm just a Man Of God, so I admit temptation, is my only struggle which I must learn how to overcome someday.

See I know masturbation is well known towards everyone, because no I will not put that on us Men, I need to find myself another Woman, or even a more acceptable Woman; I mean she doesn't even have to be The One God Chose For Me, but she do at least have to live alignment with God accordingly.

You see I'll admit I happen to Love all Women, I can't help if all Women happen to Love me back in return, I mean it isn't my fault God made me exactly who I am; see I use to be embarrassed about my Lip's, nowadays you've got people literally paying for these soup coolers, God personally gave to me.

Let me go ahead jog up to 7-Eleven, I know it must be some Women searching a Bachelor, not just any Bachelor, but a Widower too; I should leave that part out, not unless we get far of course, but when she recognizes my package dangling from my hoochie Daddy shorts, hum she'd be feening for sho.

Then she'll get to questioning Wifey demise, I'll have to say she died mistakenly, what am I saying I'm well known around here, she just better put some respect on my name:

Ya Dig; I know why I literally find myself contemplating on a daily, but that's when my 3rd leg normally wakes up talking gibberish.

See, I'm defiantly not ashamed of being myself, especially when I know I'm not the only person, who just so happens to have issues; knowing how I'm not the only person, who just so happens to talk to themself, and to be honest sometimes my conscience and I even get into altercations with each other.

I pray I just don't have altercation's like that in public, I need to go ahead buy myself another Bluetooth Earpiece, hopefully won't nobody understand my pains; well they'd notice the Bluetooth Earpiece in my ear, and well I can even shed random tears, and they'll just know I'm on a phone call.

You see, I Am Not Ashamed of the gospel of Jesus Christ, then again not everyone fails to recognize we are all still human being's; I happen to answer that specific calling of my life, when I was just a young buck coming up, and I know that nearly everyone want's to receive that specific calling anyways.

Now I know y' all think I'm trying to preach the word right about now, but cut that out, because we have all sinned and come short of the glory of God, some know Preacher's sin even worst; that may be true, but just like we learned how to repent on a daily, we just teach others the correct way to plead.

Ooh I don't hear any thunder raging, or lightning striking, I mean I can hear the sound of my late great-gramps trying to hype me up saying, boy you on a roll; though I may not perfectly understood him back then , I always knew I had to have been doing something good, couldn't nobody distract me.

I'm pretty sure we all happen to have those fond memories, which we hope to never forget, and well that's most defiantly mine; see I know I must pray even harder, because very few of my armor bearers knows me, I mean they know why I need bodyguards, even when I'm not on the Church premises.

When you find yourself PIMPING out the Sanctuary Missionary Baptist Church, I ain't gone lie to ya, it's not as if I ever meant to purposely turn my back on God, or anything; I get so many distractions as of nowadays anyhow, well I know that it's literally unbelievable, but you can trust and believe me.

Now I mean, I can't say I don't wake up with a guilty conscience/feeling bad about myself or anything, but that's when I first begin to recognize it for myself, that I don't even look like what I've been through; so because of that, I appreciate each and everything God has managed to bring me through.

You see, I know how life and death supposedly lies in the powers of my own tongue and all, so maybe I should at least go ahead, and go on a little hiatus for a minute; now I'm pretty sure that when I finally return back to myself again, I should at least be at ease and trustworthy with my own self once again.

But not up until I can concentrate on getting myself back together again, I won't ever be no good for basically anyone else, but I'm going to eventually find myself yet once again, I know I can do all things through Christ which strengthens me, and I know God won't allow me too do more than I can bear!

Now honestly, I'd like to personally take this time out to say Thank You, to all who's purchased this copy of "TO$$ It Up Production'$: CAN YOU RELATE", I'm pretty sure you expected something a bit different from what you received, but just to enlighten y' all now, God Loves You And So Do I: Ya Dig!

©DarrinDLacyJunior/2025

About the Author

My real name is Darrin Lacy Junior, and well my family has often known to call me Deeda, unless I'm in the world of trouble, then I am well known of hearing my entire government name.

On Thursday April 11, 2002 my baby sister Mercedes and I, were headed home from our Youth Annual Day rehearsal @ Greater Ideal Baptist Church, and we had a terrible car accident; where I suffered a comma for 4 and a half months, and supposedly was brain dead, and by The Grace Of God, I came too on a Sunday while singing MARYMARY version of God Has Smiled On Me.

Made in the USA
Coppell, TX
07 July 2025

51545592R00049